# SENSATIONS
## OF
# SOLITUDE

# SENSATIONS
# OF
# SOLITUDE

## SILENT SONG OF SOUL

## ARUNA NANDIGAMA &
## USHA NANDIGAMA

PARTRIDGE
A Penguin Company

**Partridge books may be ordered through booksellers or by contacting:**

Partridge India
Penguin Books India Pvt.Ltd
11, Community Centre, Panchsheel Park, New Delhi 110017
India
www.partridgepublishing.com
Phone: 000.800.10062.62

# CONTENTS

Dedicated to

The Person who took all the pains to teach me My First Alphabet.

My Mother.

Smt Shobha Devi Nandigama.

# 1. MOTHER

*Eyes filled with unconditional love and passion,*
*Lips that shine with wonderful compassion,*
*Ears Listening to your spirit with interest,*
*Smile that would put all your questions to rest*

*An Angel radiating with power of forgiveness*
*An Intellect imparting knowledge in our ignorance*
*A Martyr holding hands to comfort you in misery*
*A Healer undoing hurt and pain with tender care*

*A Miracle created by Almighty to prove Humanity*
*An Outstanding Gesture to the word Humility*
*A Tribute to the word and world of Self-Sacrifice*
*A Hermit whose noble virtues have no price*

*The inspiration of every verse written in Creation*
*The Determination ensuring there is Succession*
*The Support for every Soul in this World*
*The Strength that makes us feel Brave and Bold*

*The First Anchor in the moment of darkness*
*The First hand in the path of love and brightness*
*The Hand that held you strong to overcome fears*
*The Hand that wiped away all your painful tears*

*Experiencing Motherhood is the best gift for few*
*Like a journey filled with emotions that are new*
*Evolution of Soul, like waking up from a dream*
*A Decision that connects you to the Supreme*

*To every person who appreciates Mother*
*Be an Intellect or a keen young babbler*
*Would know, the only available offering*
*To her would be the offspring's well-being.*

*On This Day Let us salute Every Mother*
*For Being Part of one Life or another*
*Teaching the world about love and humility*
*With Gratitude and Gentle Generosity*

## 2.    THE UNKNOWN FEELING

*Your feet take you to an Unknown Place*
*Your heart beats faster that usual pace*
*Your smile becomes a part of your face*
*You glow with an unknown divine grace*
*You look forward with hope for future days*
*You feel change in many untold ways*

*On a Lonely Lane, Your Sight will discover*
*a Mystery that is lying calm under a cover*
*Which is blessed with a strange rare power*
*that can make you and your heart hover*
*Forcing you to learn, unlearn and rediscover*
*Without giving any time to think and recover*

*Your lips greet everyone with a caring smile*
*When your heart knows destiny is within a mile*
*You see every person as if they are worthwhile*
*Wonder about people who have not met in a while*
*Your heart, the Pure, sweet uninhabited isle*
*Suddenly Grows Strong and also becomes Fragile*

*Your hands welcome without your consent*
*Your legs move with or without your intent*
*Your smile makes you feel warm and content*
*Your desperation to meet destiny is evident*
*Your heart reminds you of being innocent*
*You feel slightly overwhelmed and impatient*

*You have met the One who can blend*
*With You and walk until the very end*
*Who has the will to force destiny to bend*
*With You he would never dare to pretend*
*The One who can teach you to mend*
*Fences with a Foe or a Frustrated Friend.*

*The hand that would take you to the Altar*
*The Touch that makes you shine like a star*
*The Smile that keeps you moving in a sad hour*
*The Voice that would know the words to utter*
*To make even a very bad day Much Better*
*When you are wrong, who has the courage to mutter*

*A Voice with Concern that removes your fear*
*A voice with Caution that ensures you are clear*
*A Voice with Care that wipes each and every tear*
*A voice with Comfort that tells you are a dear*
*A Voice with Curio that makes grin from ear to ear*
*A voice with Clarity that would be ready to hear*

*A Partner who would'nt break the deal*
*An Associate who would share your meal*
*An Empath who would know how you feel*
*A Sage who mends your heart to heal*
*A Solider who can take up any ordeal*
*A Prince from your dreams, who is real*

*A Poet who admires your simple Beauty*
*A King who is loyal and bound to your Duty*
*An angel who is known for Simplicity*
*A Friend who makes you feel light and free*
*A Warrior who does not learn how to flee*
*A Companion who replaced 'me' with 'we'*

*A buddy With whom you can play silly games*
*A Philosopher to share your serious future aims*
*A Victim who is part and parcel of all your Claims*
*A Pal in whose presence there are no shames*
*A comrade with whom there are no painful blames*
*A Ghost who walks into past and reclaims*

*The first person with whom you want to share*
*Every event even it be a walk to local fair*
*every dream your heart has held and every flair*
*that passed in you, not thinking if it would be fair*
*Knowing the person would always love and care*
*And To separate you, even Death does not dare*

*The First Person who laments with happiness*
*The Last Person to leave you in Sadness*
*The Strong Person when you act in madness*
*The Weak person to leave you at a fence*
*The Sweet Person who is your greatest defense*
*The Bitter person to break your innocence*

*With whom you have no reason to be competitive*
*Who when it comes to you is always very intuitive*
*In whose presence you would feel safe & secure*
*Who would know your problems and perfect cure.*
*With whom you feel always pretty and pure*
*Who acts as if he knows you since Eve*

*In whose presence the most insignificant things*
*become treasures for the memories that it brings*
*Who rides into your Memories with awe n interest*
*Sees that every hurt of your life is laid to rest.*
*Whose voice calms you in a long day's work*
*Whose Soft Speech is the biggest perk*

*In whose presence the Colors seem brighter*
*and more brilliant*
*Who eagerly captures and reads you with devotion in that instant*
*To relive that second again in future with utmost love and sincerity*
*Who would cherish you as you are in Broad Daylight and Reality.*
*Laughter is a part of daily life, not a non existent or lost friend*
*In the Journey with him even if it is to the World's End.*

*There's no need for continuous conversation,*
*Or particular words for creation or assertion*
*For someone who listens to words and silence*
*With same level of interest and perpetuation*
*You're quite content in just having them nearby.*
*With a simple gesture they make your heart fly*

*Things that never interested you before become fascinating*
*as you know they are important to this person who is so appealing*
*You think of this person on every occasion and in everything you do*
*Your world has no prominence without this person which is so true*
*You open your heart knowing well aware it could be broken one day*
*you experience a love and joy that could never leave you away*

*Being vulnerable your heart feels true pleasure*
*Yet you do not hesitate to take pain and pressure*
*Strength comes from your true and noble friend*
*Who will remain loyal to you till the very end.*

*Can this ever Happen? And if it happens, what is it called??*
*If all these feeling are to be summed up in word, so that you can explain it to*
*everyone, what would that wor(l)d be?*
*Happiness, Contentment, Satisfaction, Peace, Appreciation, Gratitude,*
*infatuation, Obsession*

*Or . . . . **Love for the Life**.*

## 3.  BURNING DESIRE

When the whole world is lull and fast asleep
But something goes down in you very deep
like a turbulence created by a stone in lake
That disturbs you and keeps you awake

Amidst the darkness on a cloudy moonless Night
Your Soul shows you a path that is Bright
You Hear Your Brain and Heart's First Fight
Regarding the trustworthiness of the Light

However Bright the path may be for your Heart
There would be Tough Times that tear you apart
Every Move may demand Some Giant Penalty
Which is not agreeable to Brain in Totality

The path ahead may need expert guidance
A willing heart should always wait in patience
Acting without Thinking may make you a fool
Inaction with Thinking will ruin your cool

Anyone who has the fire in the Belly
Will not compromise with life generally
Someone having desire and capability
Will follow the path with strength and stability

*Change is the unchangeable Law of Universe*
*That may eventually move you from Bad to Worse*
*The Fire In You Forced You to walk on a Line*
*Trust Yourself and Your Heart, It would Be fine*

*Every soul in this world has a destination.*
*Until you reach it, You have to face desperation*
*To reach which, Very few will receive Inspiration*
*Once you reach it, You develop new Appreciation*

*Many noble have earlier travelled in this lane*
*Their stories may sound easy, simple and plain*
*But remember the guts to follow your Heart*
*Is not that easy, but in fact the toughest Part*

*To reach your destination you need clarity*
*Never achieve it at the cost of brevity*
*Be Clear, Focus and Concentrate*
*Then you surely will conquer the fate*

*You are born to take this task Child*
*You would take it up now or go wild*
*The road shall always wait for you*
*And the journey is always new*

## 4.    *DEFINING WORLD*

*The exercise to define this world we live*
*is the most educative journey to believe*
*This is an activity taken up by every soul*
*where everyone would take an active role*

*For a child sleeping in the mother's Womb,*
*It is a place filled with darkness and gloom*
*When the kid realizes it is wrong to assume*
*that is place as world, would stretch for legroom*

*In the eagerness to define the unknown territory*
*the kid breaks open every barrier with bravery*
*in the process enters into the physical plane*
*and experiences both confusion and pain*

*People surround the new born child with love*
*with warm words showering blessings now*
*Hah, the kid says world is filled with affection*
*and slips into beauty sleep without hesitation*

*As the kid outgrows the space in cradle*
*would enjoy visitors and also start babble*
*but also realize the world is not this place*
*So would fall from it to define in few ways*

*Alas, the kid breaks the sleeping spell*
*and sees the things around very well*
*Oh, world is definitely not limited to cradle*
*To ask someone to define, he starts to babble*

*No one takes the kid's babble with seriousness*
*Child makes an attempt to discover in innocence*
*Jumps from the Cradle to Prove Self's presence*
*Yet, question remains unanswered in essence.*

*The baby's eyes looks at objects in surrounding*
*Discovers, there are many things under his Wing*
*Now again re-begins the definition of the world*
*so jumps again, Our Warrior is Definitely Bold*

*The fall forces the kid to take a step backward*
*or earn an unwanted label of being wayward*
*But nothing stops our warrior form exploration*
*Starts crawling in search of valid explanation*

*Next Phase, the kid outgrows baby cot*
*By crawling and Touching every item in Lot*
*The world is the room with all the possessions*
*Giving the kid a Wicked taste of obsessions*

*In free time the baby brain does some thinking*
*When it would come up with a sudden inkling*
*World is not the room but the entire home*
*To Prove, The Feet take first step to roam*

*For a toddler, the world is the place he resides*
*Reality slips in when the kid is out on road sides*
*Would make a braver attempt to define the place*
*On the first Chance, Gives world a Chase*

*Slowly the infant grows at a faster pace*
*Adding new attributes in the coming days*
*The urge to define the world is cast away*
*The desire to conquer and rule starts to play.*

*In the next phase, the definition still evolves*
*It is around the world of school it revolves*
*Later Phase, World is viewed as a place of fun*
*Making Friends and leaving mark on everyone.*

*Somewhere, Someone would introduce Wealth*
*Acquiring which Takes precedence over Health*
*Nowhere, No one would Question or challenge*
*Thus Begins the Path of Collection of Baggage*

*Ignoring the Nature's beauty and the simplicity*
*Chasing after the dreams in the world's reality*
*the child grows up not caring to define the place*
*thinking of ways and means to conquer the place*

*A simple definition of love, changed to a room of possessions*
*A sweet definition of home, changed to things of obsessions*
*A kind definition of residence, changed due to growth spurt*
*The growth has killed the urge to define and has caused hurt*

*From that day till the day last day on this planet*
*Not even once does the person make an attempt*
*To think of the childhood's unsolved mystery*
*For the adult childhood is in Past and History*

*In the coffin, thinks about the forgotten definition*
*Without wonderful words or beautiful expression*
*What Purpose will it solve, for the Poor Soul*
*That has deviated from its Path and Goal*

*Chasing Material Things may not matter in the End*
*Sticking for values might make you a Dear Friend.*

# 5.  *CHILD*

*Twinkling Stars of the Dark Night are your eyes*
*The Toothless grin makes you look cute n nice*

*Stretched ears, that tend to catch every sound*
*Bouncing Body with which you dance all around*

*Chubby Cheeks that make you look beautiful*
*Pink Lips, that can make anyone's day colorful*

*Closed fists filled with hope and love*
*Open arms asking to pick you up right now.*

*Little hair covering your scalp to the minimum*
*Little body that vibrates in your momentum*

*The Tantrums that make life very miserable*
*The Laughter that makes heaven attainable*

*The immediate kiss you give when you are happy*
*The quick fit you throw to indicate you are sappy*

*The warmth of your palm when you press my cheek*
*the cuteness of your curiosity when you try to peek*

*The attitude, that shows that you do not care*
*The innocence where nothing can harm or scare*

*The mess you create in the act of feeding yourself*
*The Things you have broken in the lower shelf*

*The Loud Laughter when you are taken on a ride*
*the expression of surprise when you see a tide*

*The way you chase after the beautiful butterflies*
*The mock expression on your face of being wise*

*The piercing cry, when Doctor is near-by*
*The enlarged grin, when you see bird's fly*

*The confused look when you cant hold water in hand*
*the victorious smile when you build castle in sand*

*The attempts you make to capture sunlight in palm*
*the noise you make when asked to be quiet and calm*

*The run you take when it is time to take a shower*
*the sweetness with which you pluck the flower*

*The questioning look when you see new object*
*the Noble Look when you understand a subject*

*The innocence in the game of hide and seek*
*When you close your eyes and silently peek*

*The wonder with which you look when it drizzles*
*The way you fight to play with the water sizzles*

*Are there enough words in the Literature,*
*To describe you my matured immature*

*Sweet Little Baby, with the Heart of Gold*
*Are you an angel gifted for me from My Lord.*

# 6.   OH GOD

*Every sacred text proves your existence*
*and your ongoing support to this universe.*

*Every Philosopher seeks you from iota to infinity,*
*From nothing to everything, you exist in simplicity*
*From here to there, you have filled with humanity*
*From birth to death, you are always in the vicinity*
*Protecting us from hatred and sin with sincerity*

*Every passing second, is a proof your Existence*
*Ensuring us we would be reaching Your presence*
*Every Step, Every Word, Every Breath is a Penance*
*That has potential to break our Dark Ignorance*
*The Path and The Destination are your true essence*

*The world is always under Your Love and Protection*
*You do not let us walk in the path of Self Destruction*
*You would never abandon any soul in Desperation*
*You created angels to ensure we have Inspiration*
*You create hurdles to see to that we have motivation*

*The Journey of life started to spread Happiness*
*When I entered into this world with Gladness*
*In my closed fists I carried Hope and Faithfulness*
*To make difference in this world of unhappiness*
*I failed to achieve the purpose with gratefulness*

*Oh Lord, Do teach me to love beyond expression,*
*to surrenderr to Fate, to discard possession*
*to understand humanity and make an impression*
*Not to compete but to complete with aggression*
*To walk forward and be part of Human progression*

# 7.    HOPE

The Single word that fights the darkness of Despair
The Sole word that can show you path up the Stair
The word that is of great use, and lightens your heart
Which Gives you capacity to learn any new Art

The word that makes you live and Forces you to believe
Which has the strength to give you skills that can achieve
Any Task without doubt, helps you to ascent great height
Shows you the source of light, even in Empty, Dark Night.

For a Leader to win an election, candidate to pass selection
For an admirer to win Nature's Confidence and affection
For an Ever-flowing Stream to unite with Mighty Ocean
For a Preacher to spread his Message of Love and Devotion

Hope gives each and everyone a fresh breath
That acts to our Life, as a new Breadth
A reason to make our journey from birth to death
a little more colorful, with invaluable wealth

*Hope decreases your despair and distress*
*it fights every hurt, pain and human stress*
*It forces you to stay up and frequently assess*
*the situation you are in and how to access.*

*Hope to reach the Stars, to Fight the Fears*
*to end all the wars, to Conquer the Tears*
*To stay safe in the moment of pain and panic*
*Not to loose yourself when you are very sick*

*Life without Hope is a life without Color*
*it is entering a battlefield without armour*
*Every thing around you looses its Glamour*
*You would be a Ship Sailor without an Anchor*

*Company may not be there until the end of Journey*
*The Path may have moments of Pain and no visible Victory*
*But still do not loose hope in your heart when you Strike*
*And take the additional Step to reach your Goal with Pride*

# 8.  DEATH

*When Goddess of Death Crosses my Lane*
*I have nothing to offer Her in Mortal Plane*
*Except the Life that I treasured, though insane*
*It is better than grieving for loss of beloved in pain*

*But Before that, I do have to make a confession*
*to make before I take leave from my position*
*It is not fear of life that drives me to this decision*
*But it is love for the one that gives the inspiration*

*No Matter how many playoffs you have played*
*Today or Tomorrow you should always fade*
*There is nothing that can be done to evade*
*But Only to Surrender with Smile to the Shade*

*Every day in the Dawn the fact dawns to me*
*Today could be the last time my eyes see*
*Sun Rising in the East above the Blue Sea*
*Conquering the Dark Night with Efficiency*

*Every Day, in the Dusk I realize a Day spent*
*Either with Contempt or with Content*
*But the same cannot be regained with attempt*
*Whatever be my Will Power or Intent.*

*From Dawn To Dusk I have travelled many times*
*Like a Student mugging up her Beautiful rhymes*
*Caught Up in Cordial Day to Day Silly Crimes*
*Dreaming, Sleeping, and Cribbing Sometimes*

*Now when Goddess of Death is in My Street*
*Knocking down Someone's door to Meet*
*Making Herself Look Beautiful to Greet*
*I do think What to Place Before Her Feet*

*For many A days I had no Reason to Live*
*Some days I had nothing to Share or Give*
*Few Days I was not ready to Forget and Forgive*
*Now It is time to enter the exit and Leave*

*I wish I had Thanked You once again My Mother,*
*For Being with Me When I was only a bother*
*I wish I had Admired You once again My Teacher,*
*For Teaching Me When I was an insolent creature*

*I wish I had Hugged you once more My Friend*
*When you promised me to stay until the very End*
*I wish I had told you once again My Sweetheart*
*Even Thousand Deaths Cant keep Us Apart*

*Alas, Now is the Send Off Time and I am Leaving*
*I know All of You would be Sad and Grieving*
*Not That I am Very happy or Likely Beaming*
*Learn a Lesson, Lead Your Life with Meaning.*

## 9.    *GOOD BYE FRIEND*

*My face is beaming with Pleasure*
*But not with Happiness I am Sure*

*You want to move away from Me*
*So, I let you go and set You Free*

*You want to Explore the Challenging World*
*By Following the Suit of Brave and Bold*

*You Want to enter the Royal Hall of Fame*
*By Creating Your Own Name in this Game*

*You want to touch and mark the Sky*
*By Aspirations that are Noble and High*

*You want to dive into the depths of ocean*
*By Touching Lives that are Dull and Frozen*

*You want to leave your Foot Marks Here*
*By Wiping Out Every Person's Deepest Fear*

*You want to Appreciate Nature with your Heart*
*By Sharing it with everyone in your noble Art*

*You want to make difference to Humanity*
*By inspiring everyone with your Ability*

*Dear Friend, Your Chosen Path is Noble*
*Yet, At the Same Time, Simple and Humble*

*You might not have time for being with Me*
*That is not a fact I take with Glow and Glee*

*Yet I bid you farewell, without any pressure*
*Because You are here to mark your measure*

*Every passing second shall be mocking me*
*Asking about you, But Please do not Flea*

*Your Purpose is noble, Your heart is humble*
*Let me not be a concern for you to Nibble*

*Stand on your Feet with Shoulders Straight*
*Looking into the Eyes of Destiny Very Bright*

*You are Here On a Wonderful Mission*
*I am Here to Wait for Your Vision*

*Let me not be an Obstacle in Your Way*
*Just give me a place in your heart to Stay*

*Let me not be a dreadful Addiction*
*In the Path of Your Goal and Destination*

*Let me a be simple ray of sunshine*
*That tells you, everything would be fine*

*Saying So I bid you a Good Bye*
*Hoping one day I would see you in Sky*

# 10. THE PROPOSAL

*Bent on your knee, Looking into my eyes*
*like I am an angel from the blue skies*
*You take me by in astounding surprise*
*asking for my hand so sincere and wise*

*On that memorable day*
*When I hear what you say*
*the words take my breath away*
*as I lift you up without delay*

*My Heart is yours, So Am I*
*From that moment till I die*
*There is nothing that could try*
*to make me bid you a good bye*

*Love of My Life, I ask you to rise*
*Let us together grow old and wise*
*Never Fall in Love Dear Me*
*Rise in it, and let it be with Me*

## 11. PRINCE CHARMING

*He wins over Every Woman's Heart*
*Without even missing a single Beat*
*His Voice and Words are so Sweet*
*They Do not let a lady recover her wit*

*With some unknown divine Grace*
*He praises every woman with Ease*
*Thrive by ensuring he would Please*
*While she dies for him to be-hold*

*With a Smile he conquers Her Heart*
*With one word breaks her World Apart*
*Like an able sales man in a Mart*
*He makes his moves with great Art*

*He is the master of Seduction*
*Who wins over with dedication*
*And is like an undeniable addiction*
*He is too fast for a girl's deduction*

*Beware Girls of Such Prince Charming*
*Their moves are quite alarming*
*They do not come with any warning*
*But they end up always hurting*

*Looks may make you happy now*
*He might seem to be really in love*
*But imagine a situation down the lane*
*Do you think he cares for you even then*

*Will he hold your hand when you are insane*
*Walk with you when you are invalid and vain*
*Trust your instincts when you are in new plane*
*Cuddle you when you are in misery and pain*

*Do you trust him to love you with pleasure*
*Even after seeing the world's greatest treasure*
*Do you think he would share your pressure*
*And always be there to confirm and assure*

*He may not be a handsome Prince of a Book*
*He may not always praise you how you look*
*But he does stay with you until the End*
*Only then He is Prince Charming Dear Friend.*

## 12.    THE PRESENT

*With flowers that never fade*
*Colours that never dim or shade*
*With feelings that have never swayed*
*Greenery from the Precious Jade*

*I wish you Good Morning my Dearest Dear*
*Thanking Fate for bringing you into my Sphere*
*And ensuring you are always near*
*For You make me see the world Clear*

*With Love for you and all my Might,*
*I went into the Forest During the Night*
*To Bring herbs that shine very bright*
*and spread aroma in broad day Light*

*Alas, the forest's wonderful scented Herb*
*With Aroma that was Subtle and Superb*
*Before your Natural fragrance, had to curb*
*So I had to again start my search and blurb*

I dove into the Ocean, for true treasure
to Present pearls, for your Pure Pleasure
I brought corals that do not have measure
For their Value on Land, that's for Sure

Alas, the Ocean's immeasurable opulence
Loses its grace and glow in your presence
They Look Like Stones in every sense
Before your Beauty and Brilliance

I reached top of the Mountains with all my Skill
Captured the Colours from Rainbow with my Will
Dancing and Singing in Utmost Delight and thrill
That, At last, My Desire to gift you would fulfill

Alas, the Colours in Rainbow could not Glow
Before your virtues, They Looked Dull and Low
My Wish to offer you something had a Blow
Now, To Gift you a Present, Wherelse should I go.

*No Flower can fight your Fragrance*
*No Pearl can outshine your Brilliance*
*No Colour can outdo your Tolerance*
*No words to explain my Reverence*

*In the dilemma what to offer*
*I started searching more deeper*
*When I ended up with the answer*
*I Felt Peaceful, fragile and Calmer*

*What else is there in this World*
*can be offered to you My Betrothed*
*Which is as pure as you Gold*
*Which has been yours Since Age-old*

*This Heart of Mine, Is Where You Stay*
*Even when you are miles away*
*Every Morning When I begin my Day*
*Your Thought brings light, Like a Sun Ray*

*With Love that can never fade*
*Hope that would never dim or shade*
*Heart that has never swayed*
*I offer myself to you My Precious Jade*

## 13.　　TO A MARKET ON A MARKET DAY

*Have you ever been to a Market on a Market day*
*When it is filled with sellers who crowd our way*

*It would be a fun filled experience on any day*
*To Be Part of a Market on Such a Noisy Day*

*Vendors aim to target you for Quick Sale*
*But Seeing the Cost would make you go Pale*

*You come to buy few things of your choice*
*and Forget it Amidst this confusion and Noise*

*You meet few people in this place*
*whom you might know from many days*

*Or it could be your first meeting*
*After which you become tight as string*

*It could be someone you teamed up with*
*to make a bargain and gain a bit*

*It could be someone whom you seek*
*To buy things about which you are week*

*It could be someone who approach you*
*As this market for them is tough and new*

*Yet you meet and greet them in this place*
*and move to buy things that you wanted always*

*Few things might catch your sight*
*And you purchase them with Delight*

*Few Things might be unwanted and vain*
*You Buy them because it is a good bargain*

*Few Things might be kept in a distant spot*
*You have to search to buy them from the lot*

*One might be an evident shopper who buys*
*Or a careful investor who dies to be wise*

*A vivid shopper ends up buying all things*
*Emptying the Wallet and happily sings*

*Alas, he has spent with all his Money*
*Buying things that he wanted Honey*

*But are these the things that he wanted*
*Or are these the things that distracted*

*When the Wallet is spent and blank*
*He might realize the foolish prank*

*Instead of buying things that he need*
*He brought things that would do no deed*

*He can go back now into the Busy Market*
*With no resource, there is nothing that he can get*

*But atleast he has time in his Hand*
*Which might give him a Lucky Stand*

*He might make some money on this day*
*and still have time to go, choose, buy and pay*

*The Careful Investor laughs at this foolishness*
*proceed into the market wise and very tense*

*He Views Every Object for Sale with caution*
*and does not buy anything in emotion*

*He might have acted very wise*
*Not buying any product in surprise*

*On his jolly trip back he realizes*
*all the purchases he made are wise*

*He does a quick calculation to ensure it*
*And praises himself for his quick wit*

*Now at the end of the day, He realizes*
*His wallet is yet full of resources*

*But every step he takes away from the place*
*May make him feel disturbed with disgrace*

*If he brought the things he wanted*
*He will not feel like being hunted*

*He was a cautious buyer no doubt*
*Yet from this game He is out.*

*Because, he has not brought*
*Things that he wanted a Lot*

*In a fear of making wrong investment*
*He threw himself away from entertainment*

*Alas, he does not have time to go back and buy*
*because in no time the market would die*

*How could he have been so dense*
*Now he ends of blaming and tense*

*In guarding the wallet's precious treasure*
*he lost things that would have no measure*

*Either You could be an evident shopper*
*and shop like a Grass Hopper*

*Or could be very cautious investor*
*Who would have a theory for every spur*

*But in reality, would you be happy*
*or end up miserable and Sappy*

*Unless, until you follow Your Heart*
*You would not enjoy your role or Part*

*Your Goals should never be distracted*
*However hard You are tuned or tempted*

*Only then will You end up buying my things*
*and enjoy what each turn brings*

*Otherwise Every day You live is a pain*
*For not acting and wasting time in vain*

*Life is not a bet to be won*
*But a Journey to have fun*

*At the same time it is wonderful Quest*
*For Self Discovery and attaining rest*

*So Dear Heart, Learn your Lesson*
*Be Accomplished in your Session*

*Let no distraction cloud your vision*
*Always be the voice with Mission*

*After all, whole world is a Market Place*
*Where we come every time with a face*

*Do not enter this place for potatoes*
*and come out buying tomatoes*

*If I entered world to spread love*
*Let me do that task right now*

*For I do not wish to live in regret*
*For not being able to forgive and forget*

*To Give, To Take and To Exchange*
*the items might sometimes Change*

*What remains constant is your entrance*
*and so do not hop in some strange trance*

*Be a helpful hand, a good friend to all*
*Someone whom anyone in need can call*

*It is not what you bring or take that counts*
*It is what you share, that would amounts*

*The voyage of new journey is not in Scenery*
*It is the eyes that see it with no hurry or worry*

# 14.  MERMAID

The Celestial Beauty of the Sea
Are you a myth or reality
Skill that outdoes human ability
Are you Truth or Creativity

The Ship Crew speak about you
Who have seen you are very few
Yet to this world you are not new
But who are you, we have no cue

The Beauty Waiting by the Shore
Is part of almost every folklore
Do you really try to Explore
Lives of the People OffShore

Your Long Hair and Lovely Locks
Spot You even from many blocks
Your Song could Sway the Rocks
and Wake up the Sleeping Folks

I wish I could dive into the Sea
To meet you in person and See
Where you are in your full spree
Swimming and Diving quite ably

*Few Describe you as eternal beauty*
*Few Say you are deviation from duty*
*Few Picture you to be very Flaunty*
*Few Define you to be Quite Flirty*

*Every Sailor carries a Story*
*About You in some mystery*
*I wish I could picture you in Motion*
*And understand your Emotion*

*Are you a heart filled with love*
*Or a Soul graced with knowledge*
*Do you always live life on Edge*
*I wish I had answers right now*

*Dear Friend from the Sea*
*Who ever You are or Could Be*
*A Myth or a exaggerated reality*
*You have special place in our Society*

## 15.    YOU

*Somewhere very far from reality*
*Where there is no harm or cruelty*
*There resides the human form of Simplicity*
*To Teach us to love and Spread Humanity*

*How can anything else taste Sweet*
*After listening to your heart beat*
*How can I feel any wound or heat*
*When I am so close to your feet*

*Is there a method for madness*
*or can someone measure ignorance*
*Is there a way to see innocence*
*Or can someone kill impatience*

*You, the Human form of Perfection*
*Who can drive away every attraction*
*You, who could be born out of compassion*
*Are there in that place with passion*

*Many roads lead me to your place*
*Which can be defined in various ways*
*It could be few seconds or many days*
*That I would meet you with Grace*

*The only soul that never judges me*
*That has the capacity to break free*
*every barrier I built and clearly see*
*The real me—for that all matters to be*

*Reside in this shapeless heart of mine*
*And teach me to make this place fine*
*Be Mine for this life time and coming lives*
*for without you life is walk on Knives*

*Every second away from you is pressure*
*the mere thought of reaching you is pleasure*
*the peace in your presence has no measure*
*You are in me, with me even in my Leisure*

## 16.    BEAU AND HIS DAME

Once upon a time
There lived a warrior
Who opposed every Crime
Acting as Human savior

His eyes show no fear
He cannot see any tear
For him everyone is dear
To protect them he is clear

He is a Gift to mankind
Brave yet very Kind
No impurity in his mind
No loopholes to blind

The Noble Soul's Love
Is a Lady as pure as Dove
Who could die for him now
But never expressed her love

A Protector and his Lovely Angel
Make the world look fine and well
By one sight anyone, would tell
There would be a ringing wedding bell

*Wherever the Soldier was*
*His Heart was with the Lass*
*The urge to see her had always surpass*
*Every other thought that would pass*

*Neither the Beau Nor His Dame*
*made excuses that are Lame*
*Not giving anyone chance to blame*
*They Walked with Good name*

*The beau took an oath to defend*
*Every Life as if it belong to his friend*
*For the town he set a Trend*
*By being available at every bend*

*He trained every person to fight*
*Both, In Darkness and in Light*
*He was there to guard their plight*
*With heels that never run in flight*

*All People caught in his Spell*
*Started learning to fight very well*
*Together they all learnt to excel*
*From them any danger should expel*

*One Day, in an untimely hour*
*An enemy declared a War*
*Thinking this would scar*
*The Warriror's Image Shining like Star*

The Brave Villagers won the battle
and Protected their Cattle
The victory reached the Castle
Where King lived in Dazzle

Impressed by the Warrior's Strength
Sent him a Wonderful Present
Praising him at Great Length
Asking him to visit Palace for His assent

The Beau looked at the Letter
But had no words to utter
His world is lost in a flutter
He could only mutter

Praise from the King is memorable
It shows the world he is capable
But it also forced him to leave the stable
Where his Life is a beautiful babble

For the first time the Warrior felt hurt
Leaving the place of His Birth
Nothing in this world could be worth
To leave his lady love on this Earth

Yet, he took the brave step again
Since it is engrossed in his brain
To do the right thing again
He tried to control his Heart in vain

*Having sent a Colorful Carriage*
*To the Lady Luck's Cute Cottage*
*He invited the entire village*
*To meet them at a decorated stage*

*Before the Noble Men of the Place*
*He Looked at her Smiling Face*
*The beauty that hunted him since many days*
*Is going to be his with Divine Grace*

*The Proposal had spread happiness*
*Every one partied with cheerfulness*
*The Light danced in joyfulness*
*The Wind palyed with brightfullness*

*The Brave would soon enter into matrimony*
*With a Lady who is his perfect synchrony*
*they Shall live in pleasant Harmony*
*Growing with each other in this Journey*

*Amidst the Funfilled partying crowd*
*Admits the warrior his love for her aloud*
*Amongst them she drifts Like a Cloud*
*At the Thought of being His Beloved*

*The day ends with a sweet note*
*Every one gives their consent and vote*
*With warm wishes, Together they would denote*
*Love and Bravery mentioned in every quote*

*The warrior with utmost devotion*
*Offers her a token of his affection*
*A dove had captured his attention*
*To the Lady with care and Caution*

*She praised the thoughtful present*
*That made her feel calm and pleasant*
*She gracefully gave him her consent*
*By accepting the gift with content*

*The Warrior looked into her eyes*
*Which do not have any disguise*
*That beautiful eyes are his allies*
*For the rest of his life, to his surprise*

*Unheard to anyone heretofore*
*He took her hand to adore*
*Said the words known before*
*That which no one could ignore*

*As Long as there is Light in the Cosmos*
*I shall not let any danger ever come close*
*To You, or Wander on Your Path My dear Rose*
*For you every word is a praise, Poetry or Prose*

*I shall guard you from Every Danger*
*I shall never let you burn in Anger*
*I shall Walk with You even in Death*
*I shall treasure the air for your breath*

*I shall Take Every Pain of Yours*
*I shall Fulfill Every Wish of Yours*
*I shall Feel Every beat of Yours*
*I shall Cherish Every Day of Yours*

*The Rising Sun in the East*
*The Birds that always Feast*
*The Cruel, Untamed Beast*
*The Sour Smelling Yeast*

*Every thing in this universe*
*Could be Good, bad or Worse*
*Reminds me of you My Dear*
*I shall be for you, so no fear*

*Having made the wonderful Promise*
*He offered his hand to the miss*
*She locked her hand into his*
*And Perfections is what is this*

*The Beautiful Lady of the Place*
*Looked into the eyes with daze*
*Lowered Her Look with Grace*
*Trying to sink in an embrace*

*He Wiped away her tear*
*he smashed away her fear*
*Yet he waited for her answer*
*Which for him is a huge favor*

*Are there any words in Literature*
*That can describe to an immature*
*What Love is and its Stature*
*In Human Life, For Sure?*

*Having Got His Lady's Consent*
*The Warrior Left town with content*
*No where in his life is contempt*
*In that second he felt apt*

*Alas, Everything that begins has to end*
*That is the rule of Universe, My Friend*
*Fate attacks everyone at one or other bend*
*How we react defines us at the End*

*The Call from the King*
*Is not a Song to Sing*
*He was asked to bring*
*So that he should always cling*

*The Royalty wanted to buy*
*His Services and whereby*
*Train Every Resource available*
*And Keep the Kingdom Stable*

*The Royalty decided to block him*
*And Keep Him at His Palace and whim*
*To Train People in and around his empire*
*And Fuel His Desire to conquer with Fire*

*After Days of Travel and Journey*
*Resting In Between at some Tree*
*Admiring the Beauty of Valley*
*He Reached the Kingdom in a Spree*

*He met the King in His Palace*
*Heard what is told without malice*
*Offered his Apologies*
*For inability to be of king's Service*

*He told King that he is Betrothed*
*To A Lady from whom he cant be separated*
*The King Understood The Young Love*
*Agreed and asked him to Proceed Now*

*With No Harsh Words escaping his lip*
*The King let the brave warrior Slip*
*From the Court to Court His Fiancée*
*To His Heart's Content and Spree*

*Bidding a Bye the King Let him Go*
*Without Any Angry Words or Row*
*He admired the Natural Glow*
*Did not wanted to fight so Low*

*But Not All agreed with the King*
*Who are inept in Thinking*
*Felt the Warrior Betrayed Royalty*
*By Not taking up the Offer with Honesty*

*They did feel quite pain and Hurt*
*Him Choosing Her in this Earth*
*Over the Palace that is Worth*
*For Millions Considering His Birth*

*They made a plan to Kill Him*
*When he left the Empire's Rim*
*To Teach Him it is do or Die*
*But nothing else for Him to Try*

*They Planned Very Well*
*Without Letting King Smell*
*Of Their Evil Cooked Plan*
*For He may Ruin or Ban*

*In the midst of the Wood*
*They Decided They would*
*Bid Good Bye to the Warrior*
*And get rid off the Saviour*

*Their Plan was Foolish*
*Their Brains were prudish*
*The Task they wanted to do*
*Is foolish Task to Subdue*

*The Desire to Live Alone*
*Not to Scumb to the Throne*
*Is a Birth Right to Everyone*
*Which cannot be taken away by someone*

*When the Warrior Left the Palace*
*The Soldiers followed his Ways*
*Sensing Danger in near destiny*
*He stayed Alert in the Journey*

*In the Darkest Hour of Night*
*He understood the untold plight*
*When He Looked for Light*
*He saw people ready to Fight*

*His instincts overtook His Sense*
*He started Fighting Very Dense*
*Not even for a second was he tense*
*To Pounce and make a Clear Fence*

*It is for him a Fight or Flight*
*Warrior Always chooses right*
*Thus began the greatest fight*
*Until Sun has risen very bright*

*The Attackers Lost their Hold*
*Having seen someone so Bold*
*They felt their feet Cold*
*Understood their life is Sold*

*There shall be no peace*
*For anyone who flees*
*From the Battle Field*
*In Hell, no Heaven shall Yeild*

*On the Next Day, At Sun Rise*
*The Warrior Looked in Surprise*
*He killed the Warriors of King*
*It Hurt Him with a Sting*

*Nothing can be done to replace*
*A Life that has moved this plane*
*he Looked at them in Vain*
*Bent His Eyes in Deep Pain*

*He took the bodies of Brave*
*Burried them with respect in Grave*
*He returned to the Kingdom with an ache*
*To Tell the King about his mistake*

*When the King reached the Palace*
*He Saw two Birds in the Caress*
*They Reminded him of the Promise*
*To his Lovely and Now Lonely Miss*

*Unthinkingly he went towards the cage*
*Looked at them Like a Great Sage*
*Undid the lock and freed the Hostage*
*That reduced some of his Baggage*

*When King entered the Room*
*The Warrior could sense Gloom*
*That Filled King's Body and Mind*
*He is sure He is about to find*

*It seems after a long time*
*The King still has not accused him of a crime*
*No one gave a Dime*
*that he is there, at the same time*

*Not Sure how to proceed*
*He went towards the Throne*
*Offered His Salutation*
*Confessed his Invasion*

*That is the First Time he heard*
*King Speaking with Pain unheard*
*King Accepted his apology*
*But told he needs some alimony*

*One of the Rivals, known for his Tact*
*Found out the King's Army is not intact*
*Having Confirmed they are away*
*Decided to attack them on that day*

*There is no one who could lead*
*The King's Army with the Speed*
*To Stop the Attack in time and Deed*
*Which has got King Really worried*

*Having never chosen Wrong*
*It did not take much long*
*For the Warrior to Offer Himself*
*As a Lead to face to Thyself*

*The King's Gloom reduced*
*His Energies are all used*
*Permitted Warrior to Fight*
*And Bring Back Light*

*The Warrior thanked the King*
*Took the Entire Army into his Wing*
*Framed strategies in one swing*
*The Brave Entered the Battle Ring*

*The Battle went on for days*
*But enemy could not move their base*
*As Long as the Warrior is in Place*
*Defending The Country in all ways*

*However, on the Seventh Day*
*By Destroying Every Hurdle in his way*
*The Warrior reached the opponents Stay*
*Killed Everyone and has won the play*

*Everyone in Kingdom rejoiced the victory*
*Which will have place in History*
*Everyone had some or other story*
*But to Warrior it is just a misery*

*The King had declared him pardoned*
*Which had made him feel relieved*
*That atlast he can meet his beloved*
*Decided not to waste a single second*

*A ray of hope was cast in his darkness*
*To meet her and complete his penance*
*However, the evil is not yet satisfied*
*He had one more Test in the Mind*

*One of the Dead Warriors' Kin*
*Aged Ten, Saw it as a Sin*
*To Let Warrior Go Away*
*Not Punished for His Way*

*He Could not understand*
*How could every one stand*
*The Person to Lead Them*
*When He Killed one of them*

*Even the Best Behaves like a Beast*
*When Anger is taking the feast*
*The Kid, new to pain and grief*
*Could not see properly for a brief*

*Amdist all the celebrations*
*When all are shouting congratulatins*
*He planned to kill the solider*
*Who killed his beloved father*

*Lost in the cloud of Anger and Pain*
*He could not think better again*
*His Tears were shed like rain*
*Everything is clouded in his Brain*

*The Soldier was looking somewhere*
*When the boy approached with care*
*But did not give a second to spare*
*To Kill the Noble Man and Dare.*

*Everyone looked in Horror*
*When the boy pulled out a Dagger*
*Covered in the Floral Decoration*
*To show his hatred and aversion*

*While everyone was seeing*
*He pulled it out in one Swing*
*Before the Courtiers and the King*
*He pushed it into Warrior Shaking*

*Sensing the sharp touch of Blade*
*Which has cut skin and started to invade*
*His Body, the Warrior's hand made*
*A Move towards His Powerful Spade*

*With a Deafening War Cry*
*The Solider turned to Sly*
*The Foolish Guy who did try*
*To Kill Him and make him outcry*

*When the Fierce Lion turned*
*His Heart has churned*
*when realized it is a child*
*who has gone so wild*

*He threw his spade in air*
*Fondled the Sweet boy's Hair*
*Blessing Him with Love and Care*
*and uttered "I Forgive, I swear"*

*The King was confused with this*
*In Anger Lifted the sword of His*
*But before he could reach the Teen*
*The Solider threw himself in between*

*With all remaining energy*
*The Solider fell on his Knee*
*And asked the King, in Blurry*
*Forgive Him and let him be free*

*"I am Man of Virtue and Value*
*To Let you Kill a Kid in my view*
*Please do not misconstrue*
*Let the child speak his due"*

*So Saying the bleeding warrior*
*Asked the child to come nearer*
*He fondled the child with calmness*
*With no trace of earlier fierceness*

*"Long Live My Child" he said*
*Resting on the child's aid*
*As his eyes strained in vain*
*To open, His Soul left this plane*

*The Child cried frantically*
*His Brain could register barely*
*He Brought down cruelly*
*The Person who was Godly*

*The place that was filled with laughter*
*Is no more visible in thereafter*
*His Foolish act of Bravery*
*Has added to everyone's misery*

*What added more to his anguish*
*Is the Brave Warrior's Last Wish*
*Which showed him how unselfish*
*Is the Person whom he wanted to diminish*

*As per the Age Old Rituals of Soil*
*The Place would be in Turmoil*
*If the Last wish is not valued*
*The Place would face a feud*

*The Warriors Famous Last Expression*
*is an armor protecting the kid in Mansion*
*No one would do anything to harm*
*the kid who is under the Warriors' arm*

*There is nothing that can be done*
*To let everyone dance again in fun*
*They Lost, Though They have won*
*Wish things could be redone*

*By looking into some far off distance*
*The King finally broke the silence*
*By addressing the lad who is tense*
*With Plain pain without any pretence*

*The Noble Soul has left his plane*
*Because of your attempt that is insane*
*He has a Lover Waiting for his arrival*
*Before her Our Grief is Trivial*

*Let us both move the Land of His*
*To convey his beloved about this*
*Let us both present the scenario to her*
*To take a decision on this Matter*

*The death of Solider is as crime*
*lying on conscience—Yours and Mine*
*I shall surrender to the Love of His Life*
*And accept her judgement without strife*

*So saying the King hugged the lad*
*Looking at the Courtiers who are sad*
*Everything now seemed to be bad*
*Few seconds earlier everyone was glad*

*The Solider had strength to*
*Win over and make others do*
*the Right thing in the Right Time*
*Without caring for any dime*

*The King and the Lad moved away*
*In Sadness, they called off the day*
*The Courtiers followed them in doom*
*Everyone is dressed in grief and gloom*

*All the people left the city*
*To show their concern and pity*
*to the lady leading a life of simplicity*
*who lost her love peace and tranquility*

*As People moved away towards the village*
*They saw two birds that were earlier in cage*
*Leading them as if they wanted to pay homage*
*to the Soul that has freed their hostage*

*People murmured at the Sight*
*Of Two Birds Shining very Bright*
*In the Sky not caring their Plight*
*To meet someone as their right*

*Unexplainable to Human Logic*
*The birds looked angelic*
*That made world scenic*
*Inspite of being Tragic*

*When everyone reached the village*
*they saw the decorated stage*
*Word travelled about the promise*
*Warrior made to his Miss*

*People shed tears at the thought*
*Expecting the Lady to be distraught*
*what misery would she have fought*
*People Felt they were being caught*

*The Lad now was calm and very silent*
*No one would believe he was violent*
*Could be because of the upcoming confront*
*Thought Everyone in Torrent*

*The birds were however jubilant*
*Shining with their divine quotient*
*They did not stop their movement*
*Even after spotting the place in distanct*

*The birds flew in the Cute Cottage*
*Sat on the Lady's arms with courage*
*Passed on the news of Damage*
*In some unknown Language*

*The lady paid her Complete attention*
*To the birds and heard them in caution*
*People witnessed change in her complexion*
*As she looked like a Ghost's Refelction*

*Never was it heard earlier*
*That A Dead Warrior*
*Could use bird as a messenger*
*To tell others about his danger*

*As the folks were wondering*
*Everyone heard someone singing*
*A beautiful song that was soothing*
*The nerves of lady and calming*

*Caught in surprise and wonder*
*People started to Ponder*
*On the Song and the Singer*
*But no one could point a finger*

*After Eternal Silence the lady spoke*
*With voice that was dull and broke*
*That could any time any where invoke*
*pain from the Soul in a Stroke*

*She moved towards the Juvenile*
*Who Looked Lost and stood immobile*
*Without uttering any sound for a while*
*Looking at some distant mile*

*With words as soothing as the Gospel*
*She Lifted his head to look at him well*
*One sight at him was all needed to tell*
*He was regretting and was in deep hell*

*With Looks that could calm*
*anyone like magic balm*
*She took his hand into her palm*
*To ensure no one would harm*

*Son I have only three things to ask*
*Answer them without a mask*
*Then you would complete your task*
*Next I shall move to King to ask*

*The Child looked into her eyes*
*That could only love and sympahtise*
*He nodded to show he agrees*
*To all her conditions in ease*

*Her questions were simple*
*"Did you know who attacked first?"*
*The Lad nodded*
*"Did you know he had to fight?"*

*The Lad nodded again*
*"Did you know he paid the last respects?"*
*The Lad nodded again*
*Without another word*

*She moved backward*
*Without making it awkward*
*She moved forward*
*She Looked at the King*

*Who was clearly aching*
*With Pain and was grieving*
*For his role in Killing*
*Her questions were simple statements*

*"Did You know your army's intentions?"*
*The King said "No"*
*"Did You Know about the Kid's Plan?"*
*The King said "No"*
*"Did You Foresee him coming between you and the Kid?"*
*The King said "No"*

*Without making another sound*
*She moved in that place round*
*She reached a mirror in the room*
*held it for support in her gloom*

*My Fiancee's Last wish is*
*to Relieve the Kid from this*
*So I shall make a decree*
*the Kid is from now on free*

*To Ease your pain and guilt*
*I want you both to build*
*A Warm place to settle*
*For family of whom are lost in battle*

*Let this place built in His Memory*
*Carry on this story and tell Clearly*
*A moment of anger and desperation*
*Will result in permanent pain and separation*

*"Son, I know you are deeply Hurt*
*But Hatred is not Worth*
*To Live on this Earth*
*Spread Only Love in this Birth"*

*"Sire, I know you deeply regret*
*But please do not fret*
*On things that are in past*
*Kindly make changes that last"*

*So saying the lady shook but stood*
*and soon she collapsed on wood*
*A strange light blinded them all*
*That prevented the lady to fall*

*Everyone left a huge sigh*
*Seeing the Lady calm and lie*
*No one knew how or why*
*But they all started to cry*

*The Strange light surrounding her*
*Made everything before them blur*
*But one thing was evident and clear*
*There is nothing to be afraid or fear*

*After few seconds, the lady was awake*
*Then she realized she passed out*
*There must have been some mistake*
*That her senses failed to make out*

*There was not a single red*
*drop on the floor or on the bed*
*Where she is now resting in peace*
*However her heart was in bliss*

*She tried to look at her hands for cut*
*Nothing is visible there but*
*Some wonderful aroma filled the air*
*telling her about love and care*

*There was cool breeze in the room*
*that is soothing the lady's gloom*
*There was warm Sun Light*
*That was making her day bright*

*The Wind sung a soothing Song*
*That ensured nothing could go wrong*
*The Light made her feel Strong*
*That ensured her to be brave and get along*

*Everyone in the Province*
*Could See Strong Evidence*
*It is not difficult to Sense*
*That it is a miracle of Providence*

*When people were spellbound*
*They heard the beautiful sound*
*on someone singing aloud*
*Few Verses with proud*

*As Long as there is Light in the Cosmos*
*I shall not let any danger ever come close*
*To You, or Wander on Your Path My dear Rose*
*For you every word is a praise, Poetry or Prose*

*I shall guard you from Every Danger*
*I shall never let you burn in Anger*
*I shall Walk with You even after Death*
*I shall treasure the air for your breath*

*I shall Take Every Pain of Yours*
*I shall Fulfill Every Wish of Yours*
*I shall Feel Every beat of Yours*
*I shall Cherish Every Day of Yours*

*The Rising Sun in the East*
*The Birds that always Feast*
*The Cruel, Untamed Beast*
*The Sour Smelling Yeast*

*Every thing in this universe*
*Could be Good, bad or Worse*
*Reminds me of you My Dear*
*I shall be for you, so no fear*

*Having made the wonderful Promise*
*I shall never Leave you My Miss*
*Having taken your hand into mine*
*I shall never abandon you like a swine*

*I shall Wipe away every tear*
*and smash away each fear*
*Being with you is a favour*
*Which I shall cherish Every Day*

*Few thought the Solider was a spirit*
*Few Thought he was a unique hermit*
*Few opined he was great Soul*
*Few Said He took a noble Role*

*But only the lady knows the answer*
*About the presence of the Warrior*
*He was awarded Heaven by Almighty*
*For his life lead with Honesty*

*Unlike everyone his heaven is not paradise*
*But is a place where she shall daily rise*
*His version of heaven is being with her*
*Protect her and Love Her Forever and ever*

*So Lord has sent the beau to his dame*
*who welcomed him without any blame*
*Thus even death could not do apart*
*Their Noble Hearts that are joint*